Is the Bermuda Triangle Really a Dangerous Place?

UNITED STATES

BERMUDA

Florida

BERMUDA TRIANGLE

Gulf of Mexico

MEXICO

Caribbean Sea

PUERTO RICO

And Other Questions about the Ocean

MELISSA STEWART

ILLUSTRATIONS BY **COLIN W. THOMPSON**

LERNER PUBLICATIONS COMPANY

Minneapolis

Contents

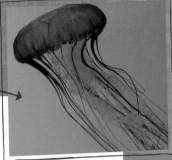

Perhaps you've heard these common sayings or beliefs about the ocean:

Don't swallow ocean water. It could kill you! Sharks can smell blood in the ocean from more than a mile (1.6 kilometers) away!

But are these things true? Is there any science behind the stories? Come along with us as we explore these old beliefs and more. Find out whether the stories and sayings you've heard about the ocean are

FACT OR FICTION!

Do the World's Oceans Really Contain 10 Million Tons of Gold?

NOPE. They contain even more! Believe it or not, nearly 20 million tons (18 million metric tons) of gold are floating in the world's salty seas. That's about 9 pounds (4 kilograms) of gold for every person alive today.

Bet you'd like to get your hands on some of that gold. Well, it's not as easy as you might think. You won't find any big nuggets of gold floating in the ocean. You won't even find little flakes. Most of the gold suspended in seawater is so small that you'd need a microscope to see it.

It turns out that the average concentration of gold in the ocean is thirteen parts per trillion. What does that mean, exactly? For every 1,000,000,000,000 molecules of water, there is just 1 molecule of gold. That's not very much. It would be easier to find a needle in a haystack!

You'd have to filter an awful lot of water just to find a little bit of gold. And think of how much money it would cost to run the filtering equipment! So if you're looking for a way to get rich quick, don't even think about hunting for gold in the ocean.

Is It True That Swallowing Ocean Water Can Kill You?

IT DEPENDS ON HOW MUCH YOU DRINK. A gulp or two is perfectly safe. But you definitely don't want to sip the salty stuff all day long.

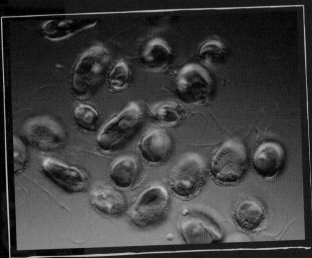

Did you know that your body is between 55 and 65 percent water? And it's a good thing too. Your cells, tissues, and organs need lots of fluids to do their jobs. You couldn't digest food, get rid of wastes, or fight diseases without fluids.

Your body loses fluids whenever you sweat and urinate. That's why you need to drink plenty of water every day. If your body loses just 2 percent of its fluids, you'll start to feel really thirsty. And if it loses 20 percent, you could die.

So why can't you replace your lost fluids with salty water? Well, too much salt can cause big problems in your body. It forces the fluids inside your cells to rush out quickly. Without those fluids, your cells will shrink and shrivel up. If too many cells shrivel up, you may have seizures. Eventually, your body will go into a coma, and you could die. So keep your mouth closed as much as possible when you're in the ocean—but don't panic if you accidentally swallow a little bit of water.

Did You Know?

Ocean water is teeming with life. A mouthful of it could be home to millions of bacteria and more than one hundred thousand tiny ocean creatures called plankton. But these little guys won't do you any harm, so you don't have to worry about them at all.

This close-up photo shows tiny plankton much larger than their actual size.

Do Giant Beasts with Long, Waving Tentacles and Eyes as Large as Dinner Plates Really Live in the Ocean?

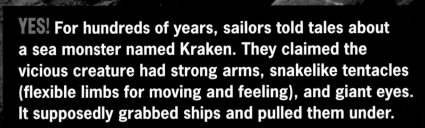

YES! For hundreds of years, sailors told tales about a sea monster named Kraken. They claimed the vicious creature had strong arms, snakelike tentacles (flexible limbs for moving and feeling), and giant eyes. It supposedly grabbed ships and pulled them under.

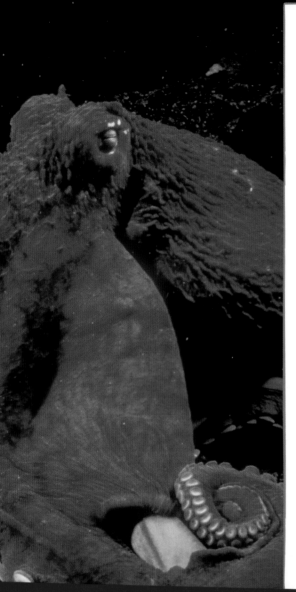

Most people didn't believe the sailors' stories. But that changed in 1873. On an October evening, an enormous beast attacked a boat off the east coast of Canada. It wrapped its long, powerful arms around the boat and began to crush it. How did the terrified sailors save their boat and themselves? They chopped off two of the monster's arms with a hatchet. Then it sank back into the sea. The men kept one of the arms. It was almost twice as long as their boat.

Scientists studied the arm. They could tell that it came from a squid, but they couldn't believe its size. Most squid are less than 2 feet (0.6 m) long. The squid that lost its arm to the sailors' hatchet had to be as big as a school bus! Scientists identified the creature with the great big arm as a giant squid. They concluded this animal was the "Kraken" that sailors had spoken of.

During the 1900s, several giant squid washed up onto beaches around the world. Each one had a large head and huge eyes. They had eight powerful arms and two long tentacles for catching fish, crabs, and other prey.

In 2005, Japanese scientists used a robotic camera to take the first underwater photo of a living giant squid. The camera had been lowered 3,000 feet (914 m) below the surface of the North Pacific Ocean. The same team filmed a giant squid in 2006.

A Battle to the Death

In 1995, a crew of whalers watched in awe as a giant squid battled with a sperm whale—its only natural predator. Later, scientists found the 50-foot-long (15 m) whale dead. One of the squid's tentacles was wrapped around its throat. At first, the scientists thought the whale had lost the fight. But then they found the squid's mangled head inside the whale's stomach.

A scientist checks out a tangle of plastic and fishing nets adrift in the Pacific Ocean.

Is It True That There's a Mass of Plastic as Large as Texas Floating in the Pacific Ocean?

UNFORTUNATELY, THERE IS A HUGE MASS OF PLASTIC IN THE OCEAN. And it's even larger than Texas.

This debris from the mass of plastic in the ocean was brought onto a boat so scientists can study it.

A close-up view of the kinds of waste that make up the Garbage Patch.

It's called the Great Pacific Garbage Patch. Some scientists think it's twice the size of Texas. Others think it could be bigger than the entire United States.

The Great Pacific Garbage Patch is located halfway between California and Hawaii. The garbage includes everything from fishing nets and plastic shopping bags to soda bottles and toothbrushes. Some items are large, but most are the size of confetti. They float just below the water's surface. That's why scientists aren't sure exactly how large the garbage patch really is.

How did so much plastic end up in one area of the sea? It traveled there on ocean currents. Some pieces have been there for sixty years. That's about how long ago people started making things out of plastic.

Bacteria break down most trash. But they can't break down plastic. That's why every bit of plastic ever made still exists. Sunlight wears plastic down into smaller and smaller pieces, but those pieces never disappear.

The Great Pacific Garbage Patch formed in a spot where ocean currents from Asia and North America meet. The currents trap the trash, so the garbage patch grows bigger and bigger as time passes.

Ocean Animals Beware!

Seabirds, sea turtles, and fish can mistake pieces of plastic for food. Plastic can clog an animal's insides. If bits of plastic fill an animal's stomach, it may starve to death. Plastic can also soak up pollutants in water and poison the animals that eat it.

Scientists are searching for ways to protect ocean animals from the giant plastic pileup. But you can help by recycling the plastic containers you use.

About 20 percent of the garbage blew off or was dumped by ships. The rest of it started out on land. It takes about five years for plastics from the United States to reach the Great Pacific Garbage Patch. Plastics from Asia arrive in about a year.

Are Blue Whales Really the Loudest Animals on Earth?

YES. Blue whales are the loudmouths of the animal kingdom. And these noisy creatures are also the biggest animals alive.

Indeed, a blue whale can grow almost as long as three school buses placed end to end. It can weigh 187 tons (170 metric tons). Is it any surprise that such a gigantic animal can make supersized sounds?

Scientists measure the loudness of a sound in decibels (dB). People talk at about 60 dB. A car horn blasts at about 110 dB. A rock concert is somewhere around 140 dB. A blue whale's call, by comparison, can be as loud as 188 dB. Now that's loud!

Scientists think a blue whale's calls can travel very long distances through the water. In fact, it's possible that every blue whale in the ocean can hear every other blue whale. So it might surprise you to learn that humans can't hear the blue whale's calls at all.

How can this be? The blue whale's call has an extremely low pitch. Scientists measure pitch in hertz (Hz). The lowest sounds most people can hear have pitches around 50 Hz. Blue whales can make calls as low as 10 Hz. To hear a sound that low, we'd need to use special equipment that can speed up—and soften—sounds.

These scientists are lowering equipment down into the ocean to record ocean sounds.

You've probably heard that Mount Everest is the tallest mountain in the world. And it is a real giant. It rises more than 29,035 feet (8,850 m) above sea level.

But consider Mauna Kea—a volcanic mountain in Hawaii. Its peak may be only 13,680 feet (4,170 m) above sea level, but don't let that fool you. From base to peak, Mauna Kea is really the tallest mountain on Earth.

Mount Everest's base is at sea level. But Mauna Kea's base is deep below the ocean's surface. Mauna Kea's total height is really 33,474 feet (10,203 m). That's more than 6 miles (10 km) high!

Mauna Kea is one of five volcanoes that formed the island of Hawaii, the largest of the Hawaiian Islands. The Hawaiian Islands is a chain of nineteen islands that stretches 1,500 miles (2,400 km) across the North Pacific Ocean. Each island is the peak of a giant underwater mountain.

If you could drain all the water in the world's oceans, you'd see that the ocean floor is home to many, many mountains. In fact, the longest mountain chain on Earth winds its way across the seafloor. It is more than 40,000 miles (64,000 km) long. The Mid-Atlantic Ridge, the East Pacific Rise, and the Southwest Indian Ridge are all part of this chain.

Did You Know?

Mauna Kea is no longer active, but two of Hawaii's volcanoes are—Mauna Loa and Kīlauea. Kīlauea has been erupting continuously since 1983.

Fountains of lava flow out of Kīlauea in short, frequent bursts and spread out over a wide area of land.

Does the Moon Really Control the Ocean's Tides?

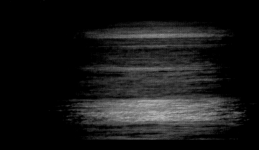

IT DOES. Along most shorelines, the sea level rises and falls twice a day. The ocean water reaches its highest point at high tide. About six hours later, it hits its lowest point, called low tide. But while we have the moon to thank for the cycle of the tides, the moon does get lots of help from a force called gravity.

All objects have gravity. An object's gravity causes it to pull other objects toward itself. The more mass an object has, the greater its pulling power. Mass is the amount of matter in an object.

Our planet has a lot of mass. It has a lot more mass than anything that's on it. For this reason, gravity pulls everything on Earth toward our planet's center.

The moon has much less mass than Earth. This means it has much less gravity. But it still has enough gravity to affect the water in Earth's oceans. The moon's gravity tugs strongly on the ocean water closest to the moon. As a result, the water is pulled up in a bulge. A second bulge forms on the opposite side of Earth.

The moon orbits around Earth. It makes a full circle around Earth about once a month.

Our planet is always on the move. Each year it orbits, or makes one complete circle around, the sun. At the same time, Earth is also rotating, or spinning around and around. It makes one complete spin each day.

The moon moves too. It circles Earth about once a month. As the moon orbits and Earth spins, the two watery bulges created by the moon's gravity move around the surface of our planet. They create high tides. Between the two bulges are low areas called troughs. The troughs create low tides.

These sea stars and other sea life are uncovered during low tide.

The Tides of Life

As the tide rises and falls, it covers and uncovers sandy beaches and rocky shores. At high tide, creatures living in these areas are underwater. At low tide, they are exposed to the air. To survive, plants and animals must have body features that help them adapt to changes in temperature and moisture.

Is It True That Coral Reefs Take Thousands of Years to Form?

YOU BET! When you look at a coral reef, what you see are thousands—maybe even millions—of tiny animals. Scientists call them polyps. Each polyp is a soft, tube-shaped creature about the size of a pencil eraser. And each one has a hard, stony skeleton outside of its body.

Did You Know?

Coral reefs occupy just 1 percent of the ocean floor, but some scientists say that as many as 90 percent of all sea creatures depend on them. Why do so many creatures live on, in, or near coral reefs? Because they offer something that nearby open ocean waters don't—plenty of shelter and food. Colorful butterfly fish, sea horses, and soldierfish are just a few of the creatures that feed among the reefs.

When a polyp dies, its soft body rots away. But its stony skeleton is left behind. Young polyps anchor themselves to the old skeletons. Over time, layer after layer of skeletons build up on top of one another. They slowly form a coral reef. Many of the best-known coral reefs in the world are between five thousand and ten thousand years old.

Many different colonies, or groups, of colorful corals can grow together on a reef. Some are large and flat like tables. Others are branched like a deer's antlers. Coral colonies can also look like fingers, mushrooms, or even giant brains.

An aerial view of the Great Barrier Reef along the coast of Australia

The Great Barrier Reef is so big that astronauts have seen it from space. It's really a series of coral reefs that stretch more than 1,250 miles (2,000 km) along the northeast coast of Australia. The reefs cover an area of seafloor the size of New Mexico. Many sections of the Great Barrier Reef are between 6,000 and 8,000 years old, but some areas may be up to 500,000 years old.

Is the Bermuda Triangle Really a Dangerous Place?

WELL, SORT OF.

A diver checks out a shipwreck on the ocean floor. Shipwrecks in the Bermuda Triangle can be hard to locate because of the deep waters.

This map shows the location of the Bermuda Triangle.

UNITED STATES

BERMUDA

Florida

Gulf of Mexico

BERMUDA TRIANGLE

MEXICO

Caribbean Sea

PUERTO RICO

You won't find the Bermuda Triangle on any official maps. But dozens of ships and airplanes have crashed in the area. And many were never found. Some people say ghosts or magic or even aliens were to blame. But the truth is simply this:

The Bermuda Triangle is smack-dab in the middle of one of the most heavily traveled shipping lanes in the world. And more activity leads to more accidents. In addition, the area's warm waters attract tourists. And that means there are lots of amateur pilots and sailors—just the kind of people most likely to have problems at sea.

Experienced captains know how to navigate boats and airplanes. They avoid stormy weather and notify authorities at the first sign of trouble. People on vacation don't always respect the weather. They may not know how to handle an emergency. They may not call for help right away. And vacationers' poor judgment can lead to boats and planes disappearing without a trace.

Ocean conditions can change quickly in the Bermuda Triangle region. Small, intense storms can appear out of nowhere. Dangerous reefs may be difficult to spot until it's too late.

A swift, strong water current called the Gulf Stream flows through the area. It can sweep away wreckage before rescue crews arrive. And because the area has some of the world's deepest waters, even the most skilled divers may not be able to find ships or planes that have sunk to the ocean floor.

Bermuda Triangle

Sailboat Wrecks

Airplane Crashes

Motorboat Wrecks

Is It True That a Sea Jelly Doesn't Have a Brain?

BELIEVE IT OR NOT, IT'S A FACT THAT SEA JELLIES DON'T HAVE BRAINS. A sea jelly is a simple ocean animal. Some people call it a jellyfish, but it isn't really a fish. A fish has a backbone, and it breathes through gills. But not a sea jelly. Sea jellies have no bones. And they breathe through the surface of their skin.

Sea jellies don't have hearts or heads either. But they still manage to survive.

A sea jelly uses long tentacles to catch prey.

Sea jellies have lived on Earth for more than 650 million years. Some species thrive in warm, shallow waters near the coast. Others live in the ocean's deep, dark depths.

A sea jelly's blob of a body is 95 percent water. But the other 5 percent is always hard at work—catching prey, digesting food, fighting enemies, and making more sea jellies.

Instead of a brain, a sea jelly relies on a network of nerves. It's called a nerve net. The nerve net has sensors that detect light, feel the sea jelly's surroundings, and pick up smells. Messages with all of this information race through the nerve net to other parts of the sea jelly's body.

A sea jelly catches prey with long tentacles. Each tentacle is lined with hundreds of stinging cells. They pump poison into the bodies of fish, shrimp, and other small creatures. Then the sea jelly pulls the prey into its mouth.

At mating time, a male sea jelly releases sperm into the water. Some of the sperm drift into the mouth of a nearby female. They combine with the female's eggs and develop into larvae.

Soon the larvae swim out into the sea. They settle on the ocean floor and grow into polyps. Then the polyps form buds that break away. Each bud grows into a free-floating sea jelly that drifts on ocean currents.

Does Half of All the Volcanic Activity on Earth Really Occur in the Ocean?

NO. Even *more* than half of the volcanic activity on Earth occurs in the ocean! In fact, a whopping 90 percent of it happens there.

This photo shows a bed of cooled lava along a volcanic ridge on the floor of the Atlantic Ocean.

When someone says "volcano," most people picture a tall mountain rising into the sky. But a volcano is really just a crack in Earth's surface. It extends all the way through Earth's crust (Earth's outer layer) and into Earth's mantle (the layer below the crust). The mantle is made of hot, soft rock called magma.

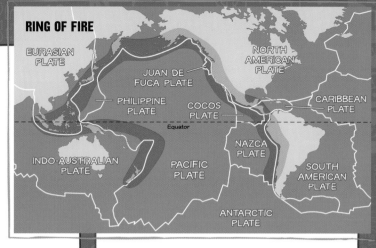

RING OF FIRE

EURASIAN PLATE

NORTH AMERICAN PLATE

JUAN DE FUCA PLATE

PHILIPPINE PLATE

COCOS PLATE

CARIBBEAN PLATE

Equator

INDO-AUSTRALIAN PLATE

PACIFIC PLATE

NAZCA PLATE

SOUTH AMERICAN PLATE

ANTARCTIC PLATE

When a volcano erupts, magma rises to the surface. The moment it hits air or water, we call it lava. Sometimes lava forms a cone-shaped mountain. And sometimes it spreads out to form a wide plain.

Volcanoes are most common along the edges of plates (giant slabs of rock that make up Earth's crust). The borders of most plates run along the ocean floor. That's why most of Earth's volcanoes are underwater.

Hundreds of volcanoes are located along the edges of the Pacific Plate. No wonder scientists call the area the Ring of Fire! Along these edges, Earth's plates are crashing together. As one plate slides below another, the rock melts and forms new magma. Some of the magma rises to Earth's surface and erupts from cracks along the ocean floor.

Volcanoes also form in places where plates are pulling apart. As the plates separate, lava slowly spills out and fills the gaps. Where are these volcanoes located? You guessed it— on the ocean floor.

When the lava comes into contact with the chilly waters in the deep sea, it cools quickly and forms new seafloor. While this is happening at the bottom of the Atlantic Ocean, Europe and North America are slowly moving farther apart.

Sometimes chilly seawater leaks into undersea volcanoes. As the water is heated by magma, it picks up minerals from the surrounding rocks. Then it blasts into the ocean as smoky steam. As the steam cools, the minerals in it solidify and form colorful "chimneys" on the seafloor.

Is It True That Sharks Can Smell Blood in Ocean Water from More Than a Mile Away?

PROBABLY NOT. But sharks do have very good noses.

A shark picks up scents from the water through a pair of nostrils on the bottom of its snout. Because the fish breathes with gills, its nose has only one job—taking in scents and shuttling them to its brain. And more than 60 percent of a shark's

brain is in charge of understanding smells. By comparison, less than 1 percent of your brain receives and interprets scent signals.

A few shark species have especially good noses, even by shark standards. These sharks can detect as little as one drop of blood in an area of ocean the size of a swimming pool. Scientists estimate that they can probably sniff out blood about 0.3 miles (0.5 km) away—but that's a lot less than 1 mile (1.6 m).

Still, it's pretty amazing that sharks can smell blood from as far away as they can. These fish are super sniffers!

Sharks have another sense that's pretty amazing too. All animals (including humans) give off a tiny bit of electricity as their hearts beat and their other muscles move. Sharks can detect that electricity and use it to track down prey. Pretty cool, huh?

Harmless Heavyweights

The whale shark (right) is the biggest fish in the sea. It can grow to be more than 40 feet (12 m) long and weigh more than 23 tons (21 metric tons). The ocean giant has a huge mouth filled with up to three thousand teeth. But don't worry. A whale shark is no threat at all. It uses its teeth to filter plankton out of the water that passes through the shark's mouth. Then the shark eats the plankton.

Is It Really Easier to Float in the Ocean Than in a Lake?

YOU BET! Have you ever noticed that when you hop into a bathtub, the water level rises? That's because your body displaces the water. It pushes against the water and moves it out of the way. Your body and the water can't occupy the same space.

Staying afloat in a lake or swimming pool *(right)* is much more difficult than floating in a salty ocean *(above)*.

If you lie very still in a bathtub, your body slowly rises toward the surface. The same thing happens in a lake or pond. That's because as your body pushes against the water, the water pushes back.

If you weigh less than the amount of water your body displaces, you will float with no problem at all. But if you're like most people, you weigh just a little bit more than the amount of water your body displaces. Your legs and arms might float, but the rest of your body probably hovers below the surface. You may even need to tread water to stay afloat.

But everything changes when you jump into the salty sea. Salt makes ocean water heavier, or denser, than the freshwater in a lake or a bathtub. The denser water is, the more strongly it pushes your body up toward the surface. And that makes it easier for you to float.

Visitors to the Dead Sea, between Israel and Jordan in the Middle East, can easily float in the salty waters.

See for Yourself

If you live near the ocean, try this:

1. Grab a clean, empty, 1-gallon (4-liter) milk jug and head to the beach. Fill the jug with seawater.

2. When you get home, fill a second 1-gallon milk jug with freshwater from your kitchen tap.

3. Use a food scale to weigh each jug. Or jump on a bathroom scale to get your own weight, then weigh yourself holding one jug and then the other. Subtract your own weight from the totals to see how much the jugs weigh.

4. Write your results in a notebook. Do you see any difference in the weight of the two jugs? The jug with the ocean water should be a little bit heavier.

Is It True That 97 Percent of Our Planet's Water Is in the Ocean?

IT IS! Earth is sometimes called the blue planet because oceans cover about 70 percent of our planet's surface.

You're probably surprised to learn that only 3 percent of the water on Earth is fresh. After all, we see it around us every day. Freshwater flows out of the tap in the kitchen sink. It flushes down the toilet. It fills puddles, ponds, lakes, and rivers.

Here's a fact that will surprise you even more: Most of the freshwater on Earth is frozen or too far underground for us to reach. That means just 0.5 percent of all Earth's water can be used for drinking, cooking, washing dishes and clothes, bathing, flushing toilets, and watering crops. And don't forget: Other animals need to use this freshwater too.

In some parts of the world, water is already in short supply. And as the human population grows, the problem will grow too. The International Water Management Institute predicts that by 2025, only about 25 percent of people in the world will have enough clean freshwater.

What's the solution to this problem? It's a two-part plan. First, we need to start using water more carefully. Second, we need to look for new sources of freshwater. That's where desalination comes in. It's a process that removes salt from seawater.

Water desalination plants such as this one in the Canary Islands off the coast of Africa are becoming more common.

Right now, there are about thirteen thousand desalination plants in the world. Most of them are in the Middle East and on the Caribbean Islands, but they are beginning to pop up in other places too. Maybe someday people all around the world will cook their food, wash their clothes, and brush their teeth with water from the sea.

A woman in Ethiopia in Africa gets drinking water from a pump. In some parts of the world, finding freshwater is difficult.

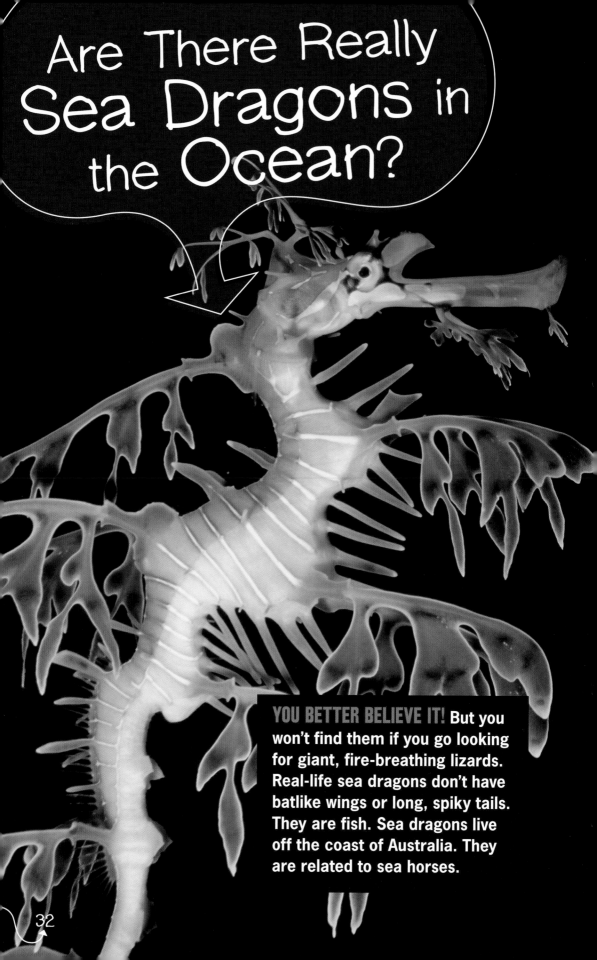

Are There Really Sea Dragons in the Ocean?

YOU BETTER BELIEVE IT! But you won't find them if you go looking for giant, fire-breathing lizards. Real-life sea dragons don't have batlike wings or long, spiky tails. They are fish. Sea dragons live off the coast of Australia. They are related to sea horses.

There are two kinds of sea dragons. A weedy sea dragon's body is shaped a little bit like the dragons in legends, but it's only about 18 inches (46 centimeters) long. Some have a few feathery body parts that look like seaweed.

A leafy sea dragon has the same basic body shape as its weedy cousin, but it's a little bit smaller. And it blends in even better with its surroundings. It has dozens of long, leaflike body parts that wave in the water, just like strands of seaweed.

Both kinds of sea dragons spend their days hunting along the bottom of shallow seas. When a sea dragon spots prey, the sea dragon sucks up the tiny creatures with its long, thin snout. Most of the time, the fish drifts with the current. It uses small, see-through fins on the sides of its head to turn and stay balanced.

At mating time, a female sea dragon produces between 100 and 250 eggs. She carefully places them on a spongy spot on the male's tail. After the eggs combine with the male's sperm, the proud papa watches over the eggs for six to nine weeks. When the eggs begin to hatch, the male shakes his tail. Then he rubs it against a rock. Finally, the tiny new fish break free. They float off into the water and begin life on their own.

This weedy sea dragon is brightly colored. The leafy sea dragon (shown opposite) has longer body parts that look like leaves floating in the water.

Do you think a real-life sea dragon inspired this 1905 drawing of a sea serpent?

Is It True That Scientists Have Explored Less Than Half of the Oceans' Total Area?

This manned submersible (deep-sea underwater vehicle) is exploring 4,000 feet (1,220 m) below the ocean's surface near Mexico.

YES. Most people think of the world as having five major oceans: the Atlantic Ocean, the Pacific Ocean, the Indian Ocean, the Arctic Ocean, and the Southern Ocean. But all these huge bodies of water are connected. What happens in one ocean area can affect all the others. That's why many scientists think of Earth as having a single World Ocean.

The surface of the World Ocean covers about 140 million square miles (363 million sq. km). In some places, it is nearly 7 miles (11 km) deep. That's a lot of water. There's no way scientists could have explored it all! They haven't even explored half of it. At most, they've studied about 10 percent.

The surface of the ocean may not seem that interesting. There's nothing but water and waves stretching to the horizon. But below the surface, the salty seas are teeming with life. Just the shallow waters along the world's coastlines may contain more living things than any other habitat on Earth!

Recently, scientists have begun to explore the ocean's deep, dark depths. Using submersibles and other specially designed equipment, they are now studying the water and the life in it in ways they only dreamed of in the past. Still, for every new living thing that researchers identify, they know there are hundreds more left to discover.

Many interesting creatures live below the ocean's surface.

Do the World's Oldest Animals Really Live in the Ocean?

THEY SURE DO! Many of the creatures living in the ocean survive for just a few days, weeks, or months. But some sea animals live longer—*much* longer.

Sea turtles and whales can live more than 100 years. Scientists have discovered 6-foot-tall (1.8 m) tube worms in the Gulf of Mexico that are at least 250 years old. It's hard to believe that these brainless creatures were alive during the American Revolutionary War (1775–1783). Now that's old!

Some giant barrel sponges are two thousand years old!

The oldest animals of all are giant barrel sponges. They live along coral reefs in the Caribbean Sea. The largest barrel sponges are more than 7.5 feet (2.3 m) wide. After measuring their growth rates, scientists discovered that they are at least two thousand years old. No land animals have been alive for anywhere near that long.

Dare to Compare

Giant barrel sponges may be the oldest animals on Earth, but they aren't the oldest living things. Some trees are even older. General Sherman (right) is a famous sequoia tree in California. It is more than 2,500 years old. Senator is a bald cypress tree in Florida. It is at least 3,500 years old. But the oldest tree of all is Methuselah. The Great Basin bristlecone pine has been growing in the White Mountains of California for more than 4,800 years.

GLOSSARY

bacteria: microscopic living things that exist all around you and inside you

concentration: the amount of a material present in a certain volume of another material

crust: the outer layer of Earth

current: the steady flow of ocean water in a specific direction

decibel: the unit scientists use to measure the loudness of a sound

desalination: the process of removing salt from ocean water

displace: to move something out of the way

gravity: a force that causes an object to pull other objects toward itself

hertz: the unit scientists use to measure the pitch of a sound

larva: the second stage in the life cycle of amphibians and many invertebrates, including some insects and ocean creatures

lava: magma that has been forced up onto Earth's surface

magma: hot, soft rock found in Earth's mantle

mantle: the layer of Earth below the crust

pitch: the highness or lowness of a sound

plankton: tiny creatures that float or drift with ocean currents

plate: one of the large slabs of rock that makes up Earth's crust

polyp: one stage in the life cycle of corals, sea jellies, and a few other simple sea animals

predator: an animal that hunts and eats other animals for food

prey: an animal that is hunted and eaten for food

species: a group of living things that share certain characteristics. The members of a species can mate and produce healthy young.

submersible: a robotic or human-operated underwater vehicle used to explore the deep ocean

tide: the rise and fall of ocean water over an approximately twelve-hour cycle

SELECTED BIBLIOGRAPHY

Holden, Constance. "Redwoods of the Reef," *Science*, July 4, 2008, 19.

___. "The Widening Gyre," for *Science*, September 11, 2009, 1,323.

"Interesting Ocean Facts." SavetheSea.org. 2009. http://savethesea.org/STS%20 ocean_facts.htm (October 13, 2009).

Kostigen, Thomas M. "The World's Largest Dump: The Great Pacific Garbage." *Discover*, July 10, 2008. http:// discovermagazine.com/2008/jul/10-the-worlds-largest-dump (November 2, 2009).

Marks, Robin. "In-Depth Shark Senses: The Superlative, Sensitive Shark." Jean-Michel Cousteau Ocean Adventures. 2009. http://www.pbs.org/kqed/ oceanadventures/episodes/sharks/indepth-senses.html (October 27, 2009).

National Geographic Society. "Leafy and Weedy Sea Dragons." *National Geographic*. 2009. http://video.national geographic.com/animals/fish/ sea-dragon/ (November 8, 2010).

National Ocean Service. "Corals: How Do Coral Reefs Form?" National Oceanic and Atmospheric Administration Ocean Service Education. March 25, 2008. http:// oceanservice.noaa.gov/education/kits/ corals/coral04_reefs.html (October 23, 2009).

Venkataraman, Bina. "Whales' Lower-Pitch Sound Has Experts Guessing." *New York Times*, July 29, 2008. http://www.nytimes. com/2008/07/29/science/29whale.html?_ r=1&ref=science&oref=slogin (October 23, 2009).

FURTHER READING

Burns, Loree Griffin. *Tracking Trash: Flotsam, Jetsam, and the Science of Ocean Motion.* Boston: Houghton Mifflin, 2007. This well-organized and clearly written book describes the work of ocean scientist Dr. Curtis Ebbesmeyer, who studies ocean currents by tracking plastic trash that washed up onshore back to its source. It also explains how ocean pollution is harming marine life and highlights efforts to clean up the oceans.

Jango-Cohen, Judith. *Real-Life Sea Monsters.* Minneapolis: Millbrook Press, 2008. This fun, engaging title explores whether giant squid, manatees, and oarfish could be the real-life sea creatures that started some popular sea monster legends.

Kallen, Stuart A. *Urban Legends.* Farmington Hills, MI: Lucent Books, 2006. This book contains a wealth of detailed information on urban legends—those well-known myths and stories about nature, animals, food, celebrities, and other topics.

Live Science: All about Oceans http://www.livescience.com/oceans Clearly written text and extensive photo galleries bring the underwater world to life.

Stewart, Melissa. *Extreme Coral Reef!* New York: HarperCollins, 2008. Using a Q&A format, this lavishly illustrated title introduces young readers to coral animals and the reefs they form. It also emphasizes the need to protect and preserve these special ecosystems.

Surfing and Sailing the Seven Seas http://library.thinkquest.org/6234/ newpage1.htm This site features all kinds of amazing facts about the ocean and the creatures that live there.

Woods, Michael, and Mary B. Woods. *Volcanoes.* Minneapolis: Lerner Publications Company, 2007. Read all about the causes and often tragic effects of volcanic activity.

INDEX

ACKNOWLEDGMENTS
The images in this book are used with the permission of:
© Laura Westlund/Independent Picture Service, pp. 1, 21(inset), 25 (top); © Rieger Bertrand/hemis.fr/Hemis/Alamy, pp. 2 (top), 5 (inset); © Doug Perrine/SeaPics.com, pp. 2 (bottom), 18-19; © JPB-1/Alamy, p. 3 (top), 23 (top); © James D. Watt/SeaPics.com, pp. 3 (middle), 4, 27 (top); © Katsutoshi Ito/Minden Pictures, pp. 3 (bottom), 36; © Iofoto/Dreamstime.com, p. 5; © iStockphoto.com/parfyonov, p. 6; © Lindebald, Matilda/Bon Appetit/Alamy, p. 7 (top); © Michael Abbey/Photo Researchers, Inc., p. 7 (bottom); © Fred Bavendam/Minden Pictures, pp. 8-9; © Eco Images/Universal Images Group/Getty Images, p. 10 (inset); © The Algalita Marine Research Foundation, pp. 10, 11; © Flip Nicklin/Minden Pictures, p. 12; © Marinephoto/Alamy, p. 13 (top); © Christopher Swann/SeaPics.com, p. 13 (bottom); © Mike Theiss/National Geographic/Getty Images, pp. 14-15; © Joanna McCarthy/Photographer's Choice/Getty Images, p. 15 (inset); © iStockphoto.com/Viorika Prikhodko, p. 16; © Comstock Images/Getty Images, p. 17 (top); © David Nunuk/All Canada Photos/Photolibrary, p. 17 (bottom); © Gary Bell/SeaPics.com, p. 19 (inset); © S.Meltzer/Photolink/Photodisc/Getty Images, pp. 20-21; © Superstock RF/SuperStock, p. 20 (inset); © James Ingram/Alamy, p. 22; © B. Murton/Southampton Oceanography Centre/Photo Researchers, Inc., pp. 24, 25 (bottom); © Michael Patrick O'Neill/Alamy, pp. 26-27; © Waterfarme/Alamy, p. 27 (bottom); © Chris Cheadle/Photographer's Choice/Getty Images, p. 28; © DK Stock/David Deas/Getty Images, p. 28 (inset); © Mike Flippo/Shutterstock Images, p. 29 (top); © Luis Marden/National Geographic/Getty Images, p. 29 (bottom); © Stocktrek Images, Inc./Alamy, p. 30; © Egmont Strigl/Imagebroker/Alamy, p. 31 (bottom); © Juergen Richter/LOOK Die Bildagentur der Fotografen GmbH/Alamy, p. 31 (top); © Mark Conlin/Alamy, p. 32; A Young Girl Riding a Sea Serpent, 1904 (colour litho), Rackham, Arthur (1867-1939)/Bibliotheque des Arts Decoratifs, Paris, France/Archives Charmet/The Bridgeman Art Library International, p. 33 (bottom); © WaterFrame/Alamy, p. 33 (top); © Ron Church/Photo Researchers, Inc., p. 34; © iStockphoto.com/John Anderson, p. 35; © David Fleetham/Visuals Unlimited, Inc., p. 35 (bottom); © Chris Newbert/Minden Pictures, p. 37 (top); © Altrendo Panoramic/Altrendo/Getty Images, p. 37 (bottom).

Front Cover: © Carl Purcell/Corbis.

Text copyright © 2011 by Melissa Stewart
Illustrations © 2011 by Lerner Publishing Group, Inc.

Lerner Publications Company
A division of Lerner Publishing Group, Inc.
241 First Avenue North
Minneapolis, MN 55401 U.S.A.

Website address: www.lernerbooks.com

Library of Congress Cataloging-in-Publication Data

Stewart, Melissa.
    Is the Bermuda Triangle really a dangerous place? : and other questions about the ocean / by Melissa Stewart.
       p.   cm. — (Is that a fact?)
    Includes bibliographical references and index.
    ISBN 978–0–7613–6097–1 (lib. bdg. : alk. paper)
    1. Ocean–Juvenile literature. 2. Ocean—Miscellanea—Juvenile literature. I. Title.
GC21.5.S745 2011
551.46—dc22   2010031568

Manufactured in the United States of America
1 – CG – 12/31/10